PRAISE FOR *IN* [illegible]

"In *In the Wild Places*, Sarah Katreen Hoggatt has provided us with a delightful and refreshing book of poems drawing us into the Wild Places where God's presence is manifested. I loved its refreshing and deeply personal insights into the nature of God and God's world. This is a great book for reflection and meditation!"

– ***Christine Sine***, *Author of* Return to Our Senses: Reimagining How We Pray.

"*In the Wild Places* can be likened to the experience of a good glass of wine — the earthy tones, the inebriating metaphors, the way one's pace is slowed as each sip is imbibed. Every word gives off an aroma that allures the reader down a path — sometimes into the very arms of God and at other times to question the very depth of the soul. This is no ordinary book of poems, but a cellar of poetic maturing wines ready to tantalize our taste buds, give new flavor to our spiritual journey, and allow us to get intoxicated on the deeper meanings of life. Grab a glass, pour generously, and drink deeply — you are guaranteed to find yourself *In the Wild Places*."

– ***Dr. Robert S. Henry***, *Pastor of Silverton Friends Church, Silverton, Oregon.*

"Sarah Katreen Hoggatt's poems articulate her relationship with God, others, and nature in authentic language and images readers will find engaging and easy to identify with. Her conversational style invites us to explore our own inner terrain imaginatively and honestly."

– ***Becky Thomas Ankeny***, *Superintendent, Northwest Yearly Meeting.*

"A gifted and creative author, Sarah's deep faith will inspire you, deepening your spiritual walk. Excelling in finding God in all manner of places, by studying these poems, we are pulled out of our self-absorption and turned toward being *God*-absorbed. I find myself humbled and surprised by the insight Sarah shares; this book will be a part of my devotional material as I strive to get closer to God."

– ***Rich Stoffan***, *Pastor of Phoenix First Church of the Nazarene, Phoenix, Arizona.*

In the Wild Places

Also by Sarah Katreen Hoggatt

Learning to Fly
In His Eyes
Encountering the Holy: An Advent Devotional
Spirit Rising: Young Quaker Voices (Editorial Board)

In the Wild Places

Sarah Katreen Hoggatt
Illustrated by Erin Kays

Spirit Water Publications
Salem, Oregon

IN THE WILD PLACES

First Edition

SPIRIT WATER PUBLICATIONS
P.O. Box 7522
Salem, Oregon 97303

Library of Congress Control Number: 2012918470

ISBN-13: 978-0-9729460-4-9
ISBN-10: 0-9729460-4-7

Printed and bound by:
Gorham Printing
3718 Mahoney Drive
Centralia, WA 98531

Cover Art by Emily Cahal
Cover Design by Erin Zysett
Illustrated by Erin Kays
Author Photograph by Erin Zysett
Illustrator Photograph by Benjamin Holtrop

For additional copies, contact Spirit Water Publications at
www.SpiritWaterPublications.com

Manufactured in the United States of America

For Christine, MaryKate, Carole,
Adria, Katie, Stacey, Emily, and Tricia—
those women who have walked with my soul
in the wild places.

Contents

Acknowledgements

Being an author is a deeply humbling experience as publishing a book is never done without an immense amount of multiple peoples' passions and efforts working together who all believe in the project. I may have written the words, but please join me in thanking these wonderful people who have been instrumental in placing this book into your hands.

To Erin Kays — Thank you for so enthusiastically undertaking this project and completing it at an astounding level of excellence and beauty. You have extraordinary artistic talent that continually amazes. Thank you for your attention to detail, your professionalism, and for sharing your ideas and opinions openly with me; they were incredibly helpful. Truly, I thank God he brought you to be the illustrator for this book. It has been a gift to work with you in this way and I am grateful for your presence.

To Ryan Canney — Thank you for being such a wonderful editor. Your innate skills for seeing the larger story and helping me see my own writing in new ways has been invaluable throughout the process. An author never fully understands what their own words can mean until viewed through the eyes of another. Thank you for being this second pair of eyes and for making sure your favorites were included — again. You are an honorable man whom I trust to great depths and I am grateful to have you as my editor and especially as my friend.

To Erin Zysett — Thank you for so generously sharing with me your graphic art expertise and photography skills. Your cover design is outstanding and it was such a gift to me to be able to entrust it into your capable and talented hands. You are someone whose character and professionalism I respect, whose friendship and sense of humor I value, and under whose leadership and coaching I have grown into parts of myself I did not dare suspect. Thank you for being there and for always making me smile.

To Emily Cahal — Thank you for letting me use your exquisite photography on the cover of this book. Your eye for beauty and how you present it is breathtaking. It is an honor to include you in this way and an honor to have been inspired by you.

To Gil George and Bob Henry — Thank you for helping fine-tune the manuscript. Your support, keen editorial eyes, and wise suggestions have been invaluable and deeply appreciated. You are both men whom I hold in high regard and I thank you.

To the women who have been God's hands in shaping me — So often throughout the writing of this book, your faces have been in front of me: whispering the wisdom I've learned from you, echoing the encouragement I've heard from your lips, and expressing the love you have so beautifully given to me year after year. I hope you understand that this book is, in part, a thank you to you.

To my friends — What a treasure trove you are! Many times when I see you, I am speechless inside because I can see the beauty of your souls and it takes my breath away. Thank you for all the ways you have loved me throughout this process: by bringing me treats when I didn't have time to cook, by inspiring the words I wrote, and for continually asking me, and I do mean continually, if I was writing. Thank you.

To you, the readers — Whenever I became slogged down in the writing, editing, organizing, and long nights of layout, I thought of you reading the book and finding something worthwhile speaking to you. Ever since I first started publishing, you have expressed to me over and over again what these words have meant to you and at times, I tear up for the honor of having spoken them. *You* are why these words are on paper with a cover and a title. Thank you with all that I am: body, soul, and spirit.

To God — You know what you did. Thank you. With every letter on every page in every book and every article I'll ever write, thank you.

INTRODUCTION

Walking through the trees, sunlight finding its way to the forest floor amidst the birds singing and the wind whistling, gazing out into blue sky above the rolling hills below — these are the wild places. I have spent a great deal of time here in recent years: walking the dirt trails, wading in the streams and breathing in the rich pine aroma of what I am sure is one of the most beautiful places God created on this earth.

I come here to hear God laughing, calling my name, or giving me a word of encouragement, a sense of the larger picture that I need in order to regain a wider perspective on what is truly important in this life. Out in the fresh open air, I breathe deeply, digging down into the rich soil, now a regular rhythm beating in my life which I have come to dearly treasure. For it is in this place I feel my soul is truly home. This wilderness has become my sanctuary.

In the Wild Places, the third installment of the poetry trilogy, speaks to this larger picture, this deeper sense of who God is outside our church walls, of the Divine light we see shining from our eyes, God's power pulsating in our every step. It's a place where nothing is mundane, where everything is sacred, and nothing is left outside the cares of God.

Whether it's the struggles we face, the delights of our spirit, or the opportunities for leadership and growth, all things along the path are there for a reason, all are gifts, but we can't see the new possibilities unless we are willing to let go of the lines we've created and step out into the wild woods where there are no lines, only trunks of bumpy bark pointing to the sky.

To truly feel the breeze on our faces, we have to leave the masks of our egos behind, the need to be right. We have to let God decide on the diversity in the forest without trying to destroy the masterpiece of river, stone, and wood. We have to let our environment be bigger than ourselves and be at peace with walking a path through a forest with a guide we can barely understand. But though we cannot fully grasp God, God has a thorough grasp on us. There is no reason to fear. No reason to not walk forward boldly.

Still, it takes real vulnerability to hear what the wild places have to say to us. But what we are learning among the trees is that it is our vulnerabilities that make us beautiful just as a rocky ravine carries snow melt down below for the nourishment of all. Knowing the assuredness of God who defines and values us just as we are, that unalterable treasure, we are free to be vulnerable and honest with each other, sharing of ourselves, helping one another, carrying no shame — in complete and utter freedom. We then no longer have the need for lines, for fences. We can run. We can listen. We can play with abandon.

Take your time. Explore the forest, pick the huckleberries, see what wildlife you can find. And you can even sit and enjoy yourself for a while on a log or before a waterfall, but the trail beckons on and we must leave what we delight in for we know there are additional delights awaiting our living presence further on the trail. And no matter how hard the path may be, or how many challenges there are to climb over, we can still come to a place of loving the challenge, enjoying the climb. We can take the strength we've gained through finding our way in the night by the moon's light, of coming to know our own intrinsic, immeasurable value, falls and all, and continue adventuring on, loving unconditionally those who also walk the trail, taking journeys with God of their own.

So come. Come hiking into the wild places with me or choose a trail of your own. Breathe deeply into your lungs the cool mountain air, fresh after the rain. Lay your hand upon the trees, gently finger the flowers, finding your way through the challenges, grow strong. Let God speak to you in ways you haven't dared to hear, the Divine touching you in ways you haven't known. We're in the wild places — anything can happen.

Sarah Katreen Hoggatt
Salem, Oregon
October 2012

Foreword:
A Great Adventure

Each layer peeled back
is a new layer born.
Letting go of the old,
accepting the new,
rejoicing in what is yet to come.
A fresh world has opened.
I close the door to the one behind,
I am moving ahead.
Whatever lies on the road before me,
I am glad to have walked
on the one at my back.
This path has helped me move on,
to find the courage
to lay down a life.
I am willing to make the change,
I am willing to make the choice,
for life is a great adventure.

A Chosen Road

This path takes us into the woods,
to living creeks where waters pour,
climbing up the mountainside,
new viewpoints to explore.

Looking Out

I look out into the world,
the cracked sidewalks,
the cold iron rings,
passersby who just pass by.

I feel as if I have trained for a play
but all the other actors are gone
and I am left in a story not my own.
A puzzle piece without a puzzle,
a star without its place to shine in the sky.

I am the rock who longs to move
but cannot budge down the hill,
praying for the knowledge
of how to make that leap,
rolling to the place where I might
find the trail I was made to walk,
streams to dance in,
the trees to climb enjoying the view.

Then the rock rolls and
at last I find a reason to look
deeper into myself
than I have seen before
and again viewing the world,
I see a road through the trees.

Leading Hands

Having to let go of
the mask of competency,
knowing what action to take,
which motion to figure out,
where to move my body
in athletic grace.
Continually guided by you,
to humbly submit,
letting myself be taught,
to be shown the way
over the rocks,
through the dust,
into the waves,
determined to figure it out—
to trek through the brush
finding the gifts in the thorns
of my embarrassment,
my own shortcomings,
gathering my courage to
let your hand cover mine,
and not to worry about what
you think, much,
but to learn and grow
in this wilderness,
trusting you, delighting in you,
finding the fuller expanse
of who I am even if that means
first letting it go…
surrendering myself
into your leading hands,
knowing such a gift will
gradually strengthen
living hands of my own.

The Wild Places of God

I walk in the night
to see the stars,
I walk in the desert
to find the lights,
I walk in the sea
to soak in the tide.

I dance in the evening
to hear the earth,
I dance in the sand
to feel the fire,
I dance in the river
as it washes over my eyes,
to reveal heights
of what this life
is being created for.

Waking up my soul to
the visions leaping,
a prophet needing
to explore the wonders
in the wild places of God.

STILL

My heart cannot form
into words what it feels,
the thoughts swirling around inside.
Decisions, choices, honoring,
reminding myself of the strength,
the courage for today.
The future scares me,
I am not yet there,
unable to live the answer
to the next question.
But you, you are here.
I don't know what to make of you.
I don't know what to make of myself.
But I want your arms around me still.

Out of the Box

They sit in their pews—
yet do not see you.
They take in communion—
but do not your presence taste.
I lay my forehead to the floor,
and weep.

Power

You don't understand
the power you hold within,
the power to
move mountains,
to lift up streams
teaming with life
and direct them
to new sources,
new explorations
of land, valley, and fell.
Grasp the strength
inside yourself,
hold to it with
tenacity and passion.
Know you are more
than what you have
come to see yourself to be.
You are my dear one,
whom I love, and I have
placed such power
into you as you've
never known.
Reach out, reach in,
grasp it, wield it
and know I have
given you the wisdom
to hold it high.

My Father's World

The trees may sway,
the ground may shake,
this is still
my Father's world.
Pain may come
and health may go
but this is still
my Father's world.
Stocks may crash
and wars may rage,
yet this is still
my Father's world.
I see this
land around me,
how darkness
seemingly has control.
I look at Him,
find hope within,
for this is still
my Father's world.

In All Times

In all times
and in all places
God has spoken to souls
and there are those
who would not believe it so
yet this most natural gift
happens to those who lift
their immortal eye to see
what is already there
and those who would
rather be blind to the
extraordinary beauty of the
Divine never fail to
misunderstand her.
And yet, generation
after beloved generation,
still we lift our eyes to see.

The Prodigal

I know you're here.
I can hear you singing
and holding my hand,
sitting where you've
always been, where
I count on you to be.
I am sorry I haven't
been listening.
I'm sorry I haven't
taken the time to hear.
But I now understand
if I do not open up
my heart to your voice,
my hand to your movements,
I will split open and
break apart, I will be
lost to the sea.
So I look at you,
the depth of your eyes,
and feel the love
resonate between us.
Whatever storms we
soldier through,
I have your hand,
the hand that will
wrap me in your own coat,
put your ring on my finger,
who will invite me back
and pull me through.
I trust you, I hear you,
I'm coming home.

When I Let Go

If I closed my eyes
and opened my ears,
laid back my head
and opened my heart,
would you speak to me
in the silence?

If I set aside
the ropes I carry,
looked up to the stars
and flew in the darkness,
would you ask the question?

If I sought you out
in the stillness,
in the steady flow of air,
would I be able to find
the space between breaths
and take hold of the
courage to answer?

Is the letting go
a prayer in itself?

The delight you find
in release and trust,
even desire,
meeting my soul
at the door,
taking my hand
to lead me in
the moment before I turn
     my face
          in the wanting.

Silent Shore

Why are the waves silent?
Why are the sands empty?
Why are there no footsteps,
no imprints?
I can't hear them,
the cry of the seagull,
the light of heaven
touching the shore.
It feels to me all painted in grey
until I lift my palette box,
unstuff my ears
and open my eyes
unleashing
the light
in my hands.

Images of Love

I always imagined
how I would measure up
to Her standards,
how well I perform
to perfection.
But knowing you
I think reality
may be quite different.
Maybe She, like you,
sees the best things about me
and helps me to see
them within myself.
Maybe She, like you,
looks at me with love
with light in the glint of Her eyes.
Maybe She too, sees my
mistakes as growth points
and admires the heart behind them.
Such deep and embracing love
flows through you
onto me everyday.
And I have been thinking
that perhaps, just maybe,
that love flows
from an even larger source,
that what I see in you
doesn't end in you
or begin in you,
but that I can find
that Love to hold
holding me.
That you in the love you give
and in everything you are,
look like Her.

A Wild Road

Everything is about God.
It's a wild road,
unpredictable and deep.
Over red-rocked mesas
or moss-drenched forests,
a planked path on
a granite mountain
looking down upon clouds,
I know not what to see
or where the path will take me
but I bid myself to walk
this road just the same.
Step by step, I tread.
Breath by breath, I inhale.
Strong and courageous,
I will walk in what my eyes
cannot see and hands
cannot touch, save for the hand
of another but where my senses
will guide me, intuition—
my internal compass.
I choose this road,
drawing its symbol upon my skin
marking me for one who dared
to go, who dared to believe
the unbelievable,
to see the unseeable.
You have guided me
to the threshold,
I walk
boldly
through the door.

Here I Stand...

...in this Garden of Gethsemane,
down on my knees in a place
where time is stilled, tears of grief
knowing what is coming
yet walking willingly into what
I cannot foresee.

Realizing all the pain
I am about to undergo,
all the hurt
soon to be inflicted and endured.
I walk into this
with courage,
strength in every step.

This cup is mine to drink
so I do not ask
it to be taken from me
but that you would help me
drink it when the time comes due
and to stand in fortitude till then.

My life is yours to move,
I give it freely.
Thy will be done and be my own
while here I stand, I can do no other,
knowing the nails will fall
and hoping for resurrection
in the morning.

Mountain View

A life is more
than breath and skin.
It's the clouds looked down upon
from the mountainside,
the wind whistling
up the cliff to your face,
trees it takes four people to hug
and everything
inside and between
we cannot see
like the glow of a soul
and creative joy discovered.

It's the grateful tears that are
cried enjoining the emerald wandering
streams as they flow to lands
enticing the imagination.
Life is waking to the dripping sun
as it finds its ways
through an echoing wood—
onto the wings of dragonflies,
warming the oozing mud.

And this is where my heart goes
when I need to remember my center,
when I need to regain a larger perspective.
So I gaze on snow-capped peaks
in a wonder I cannot describe

for I have found life
is to walk on the trails before our feet,
to hold everything dear
then to unclasp our fingers
watching it go, born on the wind
which carries us hence.

Granite Guardians

How can I leave
the forests of my youth?
Where I learned to breathe in
deep the pine sweet mountain air?
The one smell I still remember
to bring me back to me.
How can I leave the
sparkling streams that feed
into vast lakes loomed over
by the granite guardians of old?
The ones whose waters run through
my veins, are cried through my tears.
Can you cast off the skin
that encases you?
Can you unfold yourself out of
the vales that nourish your deeper life
Can you forget what makes you strong
and live without the food that sustains you?
How can I turn away
from the mountains and the valleys
to which I run for the very
existence of my soul?
How can you leave such a place
and still be whole?

Integrity

Be yourself,
be nothing less
than what I made you:
beautiful and blessed.

Walk your path,
write the Truth,
listen to your soul,
as faithful as Ruth.

You are my beloved!
Open your ear.
Pay attention to your heart,
know I am here.

The Journey Worth Taking

We come from far-off lands,
cultures apart, struggling to
understand a foreign tongue,
another viewpoint, another way to live,
to see, to hear God in different words.
We listen, opening to new sights, perspectives,
ways to love as we discover
we are unique parts of a greater circle,
distinctive expressions of the Divine life.
Yet our voices together lift up the mountains.
Our chorus pulses the river down the outward
flow into a world needing to hear the rushing tide.
We are on a journey and it may not even
matter so much where we end up,
but that we rise up to take the voyage.
We speak the truth of our lives,
hear each other and are changed.
We can love without complete understanding,
walking the light together while miles apart.
If in the tension we can find
the one light we are birthed from,
the thread through our stories,
we may discover we are brothers, sisters all,
of one skin, one laughter, music, lilting, free,
if we can just find the courage to come together
and take the journey.

*This poem also appears in *Spirit Rising: Young Quaker Voices*, a project of Quakers Uniting in Publications available from QuakerBooks.org.

Holding Me to Breath

You withhold from me what
        I do deserve
and gift me with the grace
        of what I don't.
So full of contradictions,
        you do wonders
I do not expect, constantly
        surprising me,
hiding around corners,
        in the culvert of a drain,
yet ever closer to me than
        the oxygen filling my lungs with life,
the red blood cells strengthening my step,
        holding me to breath, to love and to hope.
And you are there,
        thirsting for my words, my looks, my glance
and I don't see it, I do not know.
        Not understanding, all the while,
you withhold from me
        what I do deserve
and are gifting me with the grace
        of what I don't.

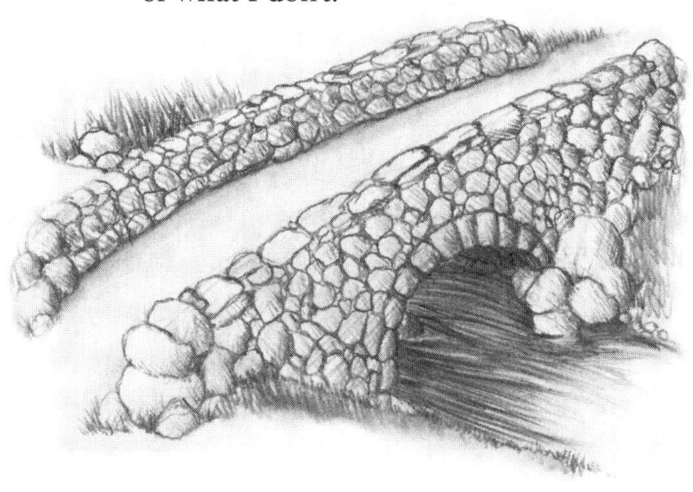

Finding Hope

Why can I not
see the light?
Why can I not
see hope with
my own eyes?
Or is it the heartbeat
that won't let go?
The breath that won't
stop rising up within me?
Is it my feet
putting one step in
front of another
or my tears that
won't stop falling
when I am moved
by the compassion
in your heart?
I raise up my hand
reaching to run my fingers
through your presence
hanging over my head,
hoping for that sense of touch.
Seeking the truth
that you are my hope
even when I cannot see you.
Even when I can't see myself.
Your breath still moves me
And that is my hope:
my hope is you.

Walking Shoes

Sitting on the mountain's edge,
watching the light leave its birth
as the shadows steal over my skin in waves.
I see in my mind the things to come—
the black water, the fear of drowning,
the tides rushing over my head.
I see the rock laden paths,
the upward climb, jagged and cold,
the view of forgotten forever
stretching out in the chilly night.
But I have gone this way before,
blindness is not a stranger to me.
I know this darkness well.
So I stare right back
into the blackness of the void,
I set my face, lift my head,
and put on my walking shoes.

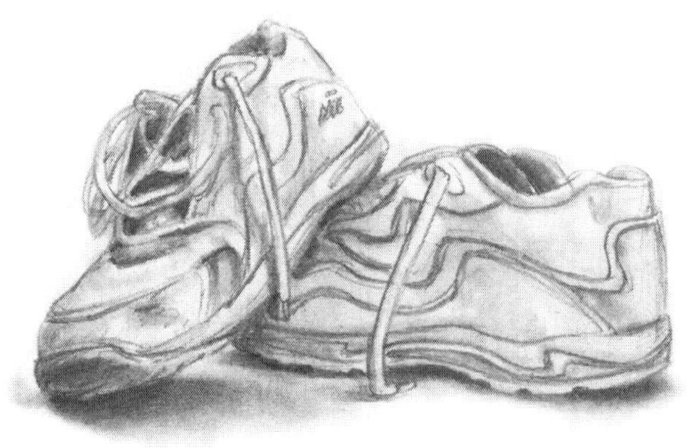

In the In Between

Breathing through the challenge,
finding the strength within,
the joy of knowing God is here,
wholeness where it's always been.

God by the Tail

God we need to
argue again.

Duke it out,
put you in a headlock.

Are you ready for that?

Are you?

Silence Take Me

Silence take me into the voice,
into the breath of words
gliding in the darkness,
massaging my soul turned to hear.
Silence take me under the only hand,
under the only embrace of the one
who took their time with me to touch.
The single touch I felt this day.
Silence take me into the connection,
often spoken of but not fully realized,
where no voice and no touch roll
like the days overlooked for
not having known what is missed.
An ache better left unknown,
unsaid, and untouched.
So silence take me.

Chaos in Order

Numerous thoughts
inside my head,
swirls of confusion
seeking refuge
in a land of clarity
and easy answers.
But such a land
is only in my head.
The truth is far
more convoluted
and complicated.
Life is organic,
messy as a muddy
ditch after the rain.
It does not give you the
flowers in a wreath,
you must pick the blooms
and brambles in the wild,
and weave them into
new patterns of
your own making
even as you accept
the patterns destined to be.
Life is not about knowing
where you are going,
it is about taking the
steps to get there,
exploring the fields
under a wide open sky.
Perhaps there is simplicity
in the journey after all,
perhaps there is order
in the chaos. It simply
looks like chaos to me.

When I Dream Again

The swirling magenta
clouds, the stars against the
dark sky forming a holy realm,
a circle of promise, of hope,
of living light
out of my reach.
But I know it's there
watching over me
for when I dream again.

Elephants

An elephant loudly
bellows its call
across the African plain
rolling on its side in the red mud
flapping leather tent ears downward
pulling up the skin of the earth
curling round onto a rough tongue
pacing the Massai's savannah.
Yet even the elephant
lumbers in silence
with measured gait
and when the head turns
the black marble eye
looks into you
as you stand mute
knowing power
is passing by.

Holy Night

In the dark I'll be there to find you.
In the dark I won't let you walk alone.
In the dark when you fall I will lift you
and in the dark you'll not be overblown.
When you cry I hear you,
when you cannot speak, I know.
When the darkness blinds you,
I'll hold your hand below.
Do not fear the blackness,
do not fear that bleakness is the end.
Do not fear this terror of night
for darkness is your friend.
I gave it to protect you,
I gave it to set you free.
I gave it so you will trust,
so you will hear the voice of me.
Wrap your body in it,
wrap it warm and tight.
Wrap us entwined together
as we enter this holy night.

Against the Glass

Like an unseen cool
hand clutching my arm,
who is there?
Is it my Beloved?
The ghost of the one for whom
I long yet fear to hear?
Is it Christ finally
reaching out to give
that treasured touch we have
stood against the glass
longing for?

Around the Corner

As the path takes
a jolting turn
and I gaze at what I
did not want to see,
I catch a glimpse of
your face
around the corner,
your beautiful smile
lifting my heart
knowing there is still
love in the world,
joy and laughter
in your eyes,
peace and wisdom
on your lips
and in your soul
an eternal light,
a ray of hope
lifting up, holding on,
laying open in my hands,
watching it fly
free into the
wide open sky.

In the Distant Woods

Hearing another's voice,
returning a searching shout
across the mountain ridge.
Waved hands in greeting,
a far distant fire
to climb to,
grasping the rocks,
winding a new path
through the conifer trees,
watching a steady growing light
as heat sensations
warm the skin,
illuminate the face,
and open up another
labyrinth in the soul.

A Moment

Could you hold me
and tell me that every
unsolved question in my life
is going to work out
and that I'll be satisfied
and not afraid,
sharing in your laughter?
I could really use a warm embrace,
a hold, a place to talk it out,
guidance on where to go,
what tasks to undertake,
sight to see the open windows.
Help me understand,
assist me to know,
speak to my heart wisdom
and the courage to follow it.
But for now, I would love it
    if you would just
      hold me.

LET IT BE

If this is meant to be,
I will guide it.
If this realm of possibility is meant
to flow into your life,
the tide will come in.
Enjoy the morning,
watch the water grow.
This is a precious time,
don't throw it away.
Relax into the wind,
hear the seagulls cry,
smell the salty breeze.
Trust the unfolding, reach out for me,
be brave, do not fear the turning,
the rocks will not hurt you.
You are balanced.
You are one, you are bold.
Let it be.

Midnight Prayer

God I see you in your chair
as if through a misty fog.
My heart longs to return,
to feel your presence beside me.
I cannot go much further on my own,
this I know, and I can hear
your voice letting me know
I can come to you any time,
I can return from whence I came.

Sometimes I do, I come
in my imaginings and I
remember. I remember
you, and us, and I cry.
I want to go home.
The other night I did go home.
I came home to you and you
sat there holding my hand
while I laid there in pain.
You let me be dead to myself
and I found you, you were beside me.

Soon, I sense, I will fall to the ground
and again you will come
and lift me up off the floor
into your gentle arms,
and though I know there will be
more pain than I've yet experienced,
you will be there; I know you'll be there
and it will be more real to me,
truer and deeper than anything
that ever can be seen, felt, or touched.

And there I won't have to smile
when I don't mean it
and I won't have to swallow
my pain and not show it—
but I can be me—
and you'll understand.
I won't have to explain to you
my age or the ages inside
because you already know.
You won't see me as less than I am.
I won't have to tell you I have
something good to give.
But because they do, because they don't,
I need to hear it from you
because I am weary of telling it to myself.
I am done defending myself,
done with trying to get people
to take me seriously
and I have no more energy
left to give to this,
no image I care to project.
I simply want to be accepted as me.

So when I do fall,
when I do come to the edge of myself,
God, lay down around me
your protection, your gentle presence.
Place me in between those cool sheets
with water and a cloth to cool my head.
Read me stories, sing me your songs
as I lay there looking at you,
wondering what is going to come of this,
when I am awake enough to wonder at all.

I can already hear you softly humming,

I can feel the heaviness
washing down my body
and your hand lifting my
head to hold me.
I don't know how we came
to this place again,
or why we always circle back.
I don't know why this seems
to be our continual place of prayer,
our holy sanctuary within you
and in the heart of me.
But I am here, I am waiting.
You are here, you are waiting.
I will wake up and find myself
there, that great darkness,
that great void and emptiness
I can fill with silent tears.
It's inside of me and all around you.

Soon the lamp will be taken away,
my eyes will no longer see
as I'm taken over by the shadows.
Yet in this darkness,
in this blackness of death to self,
I will embrace it, I will hold it close
even while it takes me apart.
Because I know you will have me in your hand
to put me back together.
I know you will be there
to help me walk again.
I know you will be there, everywhere,
everyday, so pick me up, carry me home,
and make prayer real once again.

See Me

Yes dear, I will hold you.
I will help you hear my voice.
Sense me singing in the quiet room,
my hand holding yours
through the hours of night.
I have not left, I am where
I have always been,
where you count on me to be
and if you ask me,
I will climb in next to you
and hold you,
help you know I have a good
plan for you and there is hope.
I will whisper my love
as you sleep in my arms,
I embrace your entire self,
know you are my delight.
Things look confusing right now,
you are not ready for the answers.
Step-by-step, trust your inner wisdom,
it is me and what I have taught you.
It's going to be okay.
It looks really scary right now
but don't look at the waves,
    look at me.

A Land Untold

A world untouched,
snow unseen
    out on a winter's night.
A land unwalked,
a story untold,
    silence filled with light.
Stars above unravel,
        boughs below unfurl,
    things are set to right.

Not Lost

It's not lost,
nothing is ever lost.
Like having something
precious
stolen in a dream
and waking up to find
it still there,
relieved
we breathe
in the breath God gives,
the rhythmic inhalation
giving animation
to all things,
life that is never
truly taken
but held for when
we wake.

A Circle of Real

God, I take your hand
and hold on tight.
I don't want anything
to distract me from hearing
you and especially now,
when so many things are
changing and the road is so
unclear, your voice steadies me
like a pilgrim's staff, sure and strong,
giving me wisdom even when the
choices are hard and the way is wrought
with new places I have not known.
But you are here to remind me
you are my world.
You are the sky and sea to me,
the only thing I can't live without,
the one I grab onto, the one who fills
me up as the ever-cascading tide.
And as I grasp your hand
and lift my voice, I feel your presence,
I hear your music, your words inside.
Water to my soul and
the balm of my healing,
you are there beside me
as you have always been
even if I've turned my face away.
But now I'm here, I am looking at you
as you have looked at me—
with longing and tears,
love and joy.
You are still here holding my hand
holding me to your heart,
a circle of real
in the midst of a haze.

Stronger than I

Opening up to the great expanse,
laughing with God in prayer,
finding beauty all around
in water, fire, earth, and air.

River Otters

God,
I think you must be like
the river otters

poking their heads
above the water
to watch us with
large black eyes
and then falling back
into the waves

laughing

as we try to figure out if it
was really you.

High Tide

Images sliding past me on the train,
watching the world go on around me.
Waves on the ocean lapping on the shore
and I am an island—
the causeway to another cut off at high tide,
sending messages in a bottle,
praying they might be returned.
I climb the promontory above
hoping to catch a glimpse of the
hands that have held me
even if just in imagination and memory.
Yet I am here and not there
and perhaps what is enriching me now
will breathe into you,
somehow fly through the water
to wash around where you stand,
your feet on a distant shore
and I will remember we are
indeed not islands,
that lands are connected beneath

the sea flowing on, never ending,
that you sing back to me
a thousand words on the wind
and I have never lost you.
I kneel my body down in the sand,
moving my fingers through the earth
knowing they are touching yours,
some mystical union I do not understand,
a precious togetherness
worth the risk of reach,
worth the connection over continents
of loving you at high tide
as the train rolls on and on through the sea.

God is Dog Backwards

God,
would you please
get your paws
down
off my chest

and your slobbery
tongue
off my
mouth?

Sometimes,
I really think
you need a
leash.

What Jesus Would Say and Do

Who are you
to speak for God
saying to the world
this person is in the
Kingdom and this other one
remains outside the doors?
Who are you to stand in Her
place completely surrounded
by your Christian friends
only listening to music holy
and conversing with those
who think just like you?
I thank you for following
Jesus' example so closely because
that is exactly what he did
with the whores and the drunks
and the poor shut outside
the priest's temple's walls.
Thank you for sitting there
casting labels on who you
think is right and wrong
because that is what Jesus
did while drawing in the sand
alone with an adulterous woman.
I appreciate such strenuous effort
on making yourself look righteous
but for myself, I would rather
be rolling in the mud
with those who are outside
your circle — the kind,
the welcoming and generous,
the decorated lovers with

open arms accepting
all those who tug
on their robes in the streets
and who eat and party
with fellow "sinners."
If I am wrong for communing
over a ruby beer or sharing
friendship with those you
deem unclean, let the punishment
rain down on my own head for
I would rather error
across the line of love
than sit in the seat of judgment
and condemnation
which was never mine to give
but only to take for having
dealt it out first.
We will be judged by our
own rules so I will govern myself
by the law of grace
and let you be guided
by what you think
Jesus would say and do.

I'll Stare at the Sky

I'll spread out a blanket
on the rolling hills
and stare up at the sky.
I'll think of little bugs,
towering trees and
ride a roving river into your hands.
Lying there, I'll lose
myself into the depth of blue,
find the moon hanging
in the day beside the sun.
You reaching out from one cloud
and I reaching from another,
we'll touch, we'll reach,
you'll smile and I'll remember

at last the memory of music,
the memory of my Spirit
losing its way treading the stars.
We'll find the galaxy I sought,
I'll see the heart of the world,
the points of light all lights
are hung from.
I'll take these guides as my own,
I'll speak to them and they to me
and I will no longer be lost or afraid,
I'll be found and you'll be here.
I'll see your fingers, your grasp,
your eyes, and you'll whisper
what my soul can only understand,
the nourishing words
to make me whole
and we'll laugh and giggle.
You'll blow dandelion seeds
into the wind and tell jokes
about skeletons and chickens
crossing roads and I'll
erupt in torrents of laughter.
We'll revel in the warmth
on our faces, in the smell of the grass,
and then we'll sink
back into the grassland,
under the everlasting sea
flowing above us and through us
and know we've come home,
staring at the sky.

Nothing Held Back

God, I am here sitting in this wilderness
choked up with words unsaid,
scared of your reaction
for the sentences aren't pretty
or even very worshipful right now.
In fact, I am quite mad
and I'm frustrated with you
but I don't want to tell you
because I think you would be
mad right back at me.
So I am here to pray but I
just can't find the right words.
What do you think the right words are?
Words of praise, telling you how great you are,
how wonderful is this world that you made.
But you aren't thinking that
right now are you?
No, I'm really not.
I don't know what you think
you're doing but I don't like it.
You have it all wrong!
And you are mad at me about it.
Yes, I am really angry with you,
infuriated even!
Wait! I didn't mean to say that!
Oh, yes, you did!
You're infuriated with me.
You don't like what is going on
and I understand and hear what you're saying.
Are you going to smite me?
Smite you? For what?
For being angry with you.
Of course not!

First of all, I don't "smite."
Second of all, I'm not angry at you.
You being angry with me *does not*
automatically make me angry with you.
It doesn't? Why not?
I would rather have a real relationship with you
where you say exactly what you're thinking,
where you're honest with me instead of
hearing what you say and
knowing you're not telling me the truth.
I would rather know the real you!
Do you like it when your friends lie to you*?*
Well, no…
Neither do I.
I can take it when you're glad
and I can definitely take it when you're angry.
I'm an extraordinarily big God.
I want to know all *of you,*
not just the parts you're happy with.
And you can't know all of me
unless you're open with all of you.
So I can tell you everything?
Really? Even how angry I am?
Especially how angry you are.
I want to hear it all. Pour it out,
leave it all within me.
Okay. Well, to begin with…

Fire Blitz

When the world seems
to be cast in shadow
and the flames of despair
are burning all around you,
there is no place to run—
          but to God.

Though the heat of the fire
storm roars and rages,
as you are being burned
by the scorching winds,
know you are being driven—
          to God.

Though you may not see,
though your face
may be caked with soot
and your hands
are fallen red at your side,
take heart—
lift up your eyes
to the cathedral dome
     and see the
          eyes of God.

Knowing the Stars

Lying on my back looking up at the stars,
I can feel you lying beside me
quietly gazing at the wonders you made.
Cool gentle breezes flow over us
whispering through the grass,
opening us to the expanses above,
reaching down to touch our faces as we are
held up by the world below.
The darkness wraps us in stillness
in a moment beyond time,
beyond understanding, beyond
my comprehension of anything
I have yet seen and heard.
It is a world quite apart
or deep within,
a quiet place filled with holy wonder
where nothing seems to matter
beyond just lying here with you,
just knowing the feel of your presence
making me whole, filled, beloved.
Feeling your warm breath on my cheek,
your fingers entwining my hands,
I remember what it is to rely on the One
who is my light and my sun,
the one who teaches me to take joy in the darkness,
through the times sight is short and
questions are long in coming,
the times when I see what is truly there.
I remember what I too often forget,
that you are written in the stars we are guided by,
that the stars are the same no matter where you lie,
and that we could be on the highest field as we are now
or in the lowest ravine as we have sometimes been.

I wish it was easier for me to come here,
easier to triumph over my shame and join you,
to lose my own judgment,
my own limited sense of self.
For when I am looking at the stars with you
I can sense the deep expanse is who I am inside,
my true self, divine and endlessly beautiful
as you are divinely endless and beautiful.
So on this night as we lie and gaze at your stars, our stars,
help me in the silence to really see them,
to feel that deep connection flowing through me,
everything you are into everything we are,
that reality beyond what I can describe,
the reality lit up and guided by the stars above,
the reality I want to know with you.
Then maybe if you grant me this grace,
the angels will find me worshipping here,
they'll find me looking at the stars
and they will tell me to follow them.
They will tell me about moments and
beautiful salvations that will take my
breath away and they will give me breath to
breathe you in and to breathe you out.
They will come one day soon,
they will come into the silence and they will sing
magnificent songs my soul will understand.
I know they will come and greet us,
they will come and wrap us in glorious grace.
And when they guide me as I know they will,
when they point the way in the sky,
the divine way you have given me,
I will arise, I will lift up my eyes,
and as in ages not so long ago,
in a field not so far away,
I, too, will dare to walk the world above
and I, too, shall follow the stars.

THE DEEPER REAL

You see what I can see,
you hear what I can hear.
You speak what my soul
struggles to find the words to utter,
the things beyond the shadows,
beyond the curvature of field
and hill, beyond the touch of breath.
And yet your soul also walks
these dales hidden to reason,
hidden to all those who only
see the trees and never
the pulse of spirit within them
to which branches dance
and the soil sings
and I, I call out in lifted voice
to join the wordless song
humming through the wind
reverberating through the ground
of this world you call invisible
but to me and I am sure to you,
is the most real thing,
the most visible and most congruous,
the deepest rhythms,
the highest energy—
fields connecting,
never separating,
always pointing
to the widening connection,
the deeper real—
born in us all.

Your Own Wine

You could be eating a
feast at your own table
and yet you lie underneath the
tables of others hoping
some morsels of crumbs will
fall to the floor but they don't
and you are a fool—
a fool to think they ever will.
They never will give you what you seek,
why do you keep looking?
Why do you wait for what
will never come?
Go home and pull out your own chair,
pour yourself a glass of wine
into your own cup
and eat your own bread.
Rest your feet—
find your own path.
Eat your fill and look
for what is already yours:
a meal set before you,
rich and sweet,
just waiting to be discovered.

Desert Water

Fearless to say
I need to pray,
struggling
down on my knees
with a God
not always easy to see.
Yet I raise my face
to say I am his,
knowing the deepest
part of me is
all about her.
For this feeling well
remembered,
water longed for
in the dry heat of the
drought of summer
is the gift I gather
as the tears fall,
hearing the echoed words
of a language I can only
utter among the drifts,
crying with joy to hear it again.
Your voice washing over me,
lifting my face to the shower,
of truth, cascading love,
of this grace who knew me before
and sees me now, knowing
who I'm becoming,
delight in your eyes as I find the
words to say I love you,
to say I remember our times
together soaking in these desert
sands, how much they've meant
to me and how much they still do
when I come to my knees again.

Above Eternity

Lying on my back upon this hill
out in the cold night air,
I hear your voice in the rustling grass
when I lift my breath in prayer.

Out in the dark around the moon,
no one here but you,
your wisdom speaks inside me,
calling my name anew.

Diving down into the stars,
light calls forth to light,
divine within responding
to worlds beyond my sight.

Colors washing over my skin,
exploding space, floods down,
no division between us now,
we are one, together drown.

Quiet Space

Quiet space,
    I've come to thee.
Quiet space,
    I rest in thee.
I shut you out,
    cast you aside,
but I need your silence,
    in you to abide.
The noises had come,
    the noises are gone.
I can't keep living
    without hearing your song.
I need to breathe,
    to relax in a chair,
to stop and to think
    with you around me there.
Too much has gone on
    as I've raced through,
that I forgot the value,
    the value of you.
I hurried for others
    but forgot my own soul.
I busied myself so as
    to not see the hole
of everything missing,
    of what I left out,
until it had had it
    and let out a shout!
And I had to stop,
    to stand where I stood,
to pack up my bags
    and head to the wood.
Now I can see

the need for a change,
for life to be different,
time rearranged.
What I've been doing,
it all matters not
if I leave out
what I've been taught—
that I am here
to be what you made,
a writer, your friend,
a life loved and obeyed.
So I alter my course,
from here it is new,
I'll relearn how to listen
to myself and to you.
I'll take the time,
learn to say "no,"
I'll stop being busy
for I have missed you so.
A soul cannot live
without room to breathe.
A soul cannot grow
without room to perceive
the God who is here
with no in-between,
speaking now in the silence,
who can always be seen.

So quiet space,
I've come to be.
Quiet space,
I rest in thee.

Human Becoming

Carving us into truer selves,
seeking out what can't be seen,
reveling in the changing power,
calling out what's always been.

On the Shores

On the shores of my
redemption,
treading on the sands
of salvation,
I walk into you,
feeling you rush
through my body,
my soul returning
to the source of my spirit,
the love to which all
things are drawn,
all beings find their home
and I know my true self.

Body Beautiful

Birthed from
sun falling upon
shoulders unadorned
and I am not ashamed.
These waters I am birthed from,
this gift I've been given
of my body, heart beating
beautiful and whole
and the rays smile down
on my bare skin,
delighting in my play.
My gasp of cold pleasure
sinking down into the water
flowing over the stones,
the current pulling my toes
caressing over my arms,
Mother God reminding me
I am hers, made out of her image,
shaped by the water,
unfolding as the leaves overhead
dancing upon their branches
in the sweet westward wind.

Naked Bodies in the Louvre

Walking the grand halls
of the famous Louvre Museum,
soaking in the artistic
expressions of the ages,
marble sculptures,
canvases striking one
in wonder, the subjects
standing tall and strong—
proud to be human,
to have a body:
curved stomachs, wide hips,
a bare back, chest to the sun.
They lounge with one
another, they lie apart,
wrapped in a rapt embrace
or upright with a daring gaze.

The steady eyes challenge the
viewer to look at themselves,
as a gauntlet thrown
to value in a new way,
bold and brazen,
the joys of physical being,
our bodies, our movements,
redefining our judgment,
declaring beautiful
what is truly sacred.

They stand,
they hang on the wall,
reflecting back to us
in artistic language
everything
we need to see.

From Time into Reality

This unseen life where
God moves beyond our grasp
such as the aura of a soul,
an energy field
unique to the body
humming in the air,
breathing in, breathing
on another, radiating
color, an aqua marine green
pulsating roots into the earth
sparkling with Divine light
into unheard singing,
an aria to the womb of power
where time ends and
reality begins,
that catches us like the
invisible scent of pine or
the unfelt touch of a hand
tingling down my back
in unforeseen knowledge,
wrapping my spirit to raise
itself, to open my mind
to see with my heart,
for I've walked the beach
of this physical globe
and can see the whole
world opens up after the shore.

The Heavens Drummed

Flames burn, shadows leap upon
the dancing ripples of skin,
jumping in God
as the heavens drum.
A soul walks free,
a spirit flies
straight to the skies
where light bursts
through the clouds.
The rhythm is steady,
we shout in the rain
and the Lord is glad
    as the heavens
        drum.

No Matter Where We Are

I don't see the plan,
the way things all should go.
I thought I knew which road to take
but there were things I didn't know.
I didn't know this road would come,
I didn't know the turn,
I didn't know the dream I'd left
would find me, one day return.
Now I stand with bated breath,
the choice is yet to make.
Do I follow what I planned
and give what you let me take?
Do I continue to follow your call,
the voice I thought I heard?
Was it really you who spoke
or was it my own word?
But for right now, we'll have to see
where this road may lead,
who knows but this may be
what you know I need?
So I change my steps
far from the trail I'd planned
and take an all new lighted path
flowing from your hand.
Though I cannot pretend to see
what this path will mean,
I will take a chance on life
knowing I am seen
by you the one I'll ever love
who has guided me thus far,
and you will bring me to what is best
no matter where we are.

Peace

Peace, you say.
I'm not feeling very peaceful, God.
Why not?
Sometimes it feels like all my
familiar surroundings are breaking apart,
what I treasure slips away
like so many leaves down a stream
even as I am reaching for them
and I have a hard time
finding that peaceful place
where I'm okay with what I love leaving.
I will always be here.
Yes, I know you're still here
and I am grateful,
you are who I look to for constancy.
So why are you upset?
Because I grieve for them.
I hear what you're saying,
that the lack of conflict
is not what peace is
but it can be hard to find
when you feel like you've
taken one hit after another
however trivial several may be
and I know some of those losses
are my own fault,
born out of mistakes I've made
and I'm working on forgiving myself
but it's not easy.
Peace.
Peace, you say.
Did you have peace
when you were mad?
Did you have peace as you

were overturning tables in the temple?
Can you be angry and peaceful
at the same time?
What is peace about anyway?
Is it being okay with everything
going on because let me tell you,
I'm not okay with it.
In case you haven't noticed,
there are some awful things
going on here and I don't
have peace about them.
      Peace.
Why? Why have peace?
Why think everything is okay
when I am hurting and they are hurting
and the hurt is not just going
to get up and walk away?
      Peace.
Peace isn't easy God.
Do you know that?
It's hard won—
you have to fall flat on your face—
a lot — to know life goes on
beyond the hurt.
You have to walk through the pain
to know the existence of joy within it.
You have to be willing to look at yourself,
perceived flaws and talents taken together,
to know the presence of you
and to be okay with *your* power
giving life to *my* power—
the power of the peace you give.
Don't you remember how hard that is?
But still, you insist on peace.
Peace when I fall, peace when I get up,
peace in joy and peace in hardships.

How do you have peace in
all these different experiences?
When they bring so many different
feelings along with them?
And as you may guess, peace is usually
not the first in line among those emotions.
How do you pull in peace among that crowd?
Peace is not one of many.
Nor is peace being okay
with the hard things
but it is knowing there is something
greater beyond the challenges.
I — I am your peace.
I am greater than anything
you will ever encounter.
Your relationship with me—
there is your peace.
Your peace is seeing the larger picture
and knowing who created it.
Oh. What about when I fall?
Lesson learned. Well done!
When I feel overwhelmed?
Look at me. I'll remind you of your peace.
What about when I can't see you?
It doesn't mean I'm not there.
Peace lives inside you.
It's what keeps you steady;
it's the ballast in your boat.
And you know what?
You already live it out — you're whole!
I see it every day.
So peace is being complete in you
and sharing it with the world.
Yes, and you know that.
You're right, I do. But I need to be reminded.
I know.

Heartbeat of a Dragon

Standing tall,
my eye on the waves,
the currents lapping on the shore,
feeling the heartbeat of a dragon
beating before me,
rising up through my feet
into my hands as I guide
a boat sure and strong.
Paddles hit the water
in rhythmic time,
moving in one motion.
Forward and back,
together, united,
an explosion of power
launching us forward.
A team—
each person one of many,
for one purpose — one joy.
Apart, we can do nothing
but in synch, each taking a bench
we can be so much more:
a living, breathing dragon
    coursing the waves
        as one.

Seeking

I close my eyes
in the light of the sun,
tune my heart to the darkness,
the great emptiness
full of who you are,
floating, falling,
holding to your voice,
seeking you out,
voicing my own inner heart,
my own divinity,
the image of you
always in me,
the spark that seeks you out
and does not rest
until it hears
your whispered words
echoing in my soul.
I know you also
unfold yourself
in the splendor of light
but when the lights dim,
my senses are open
and your light
shines the brighter.

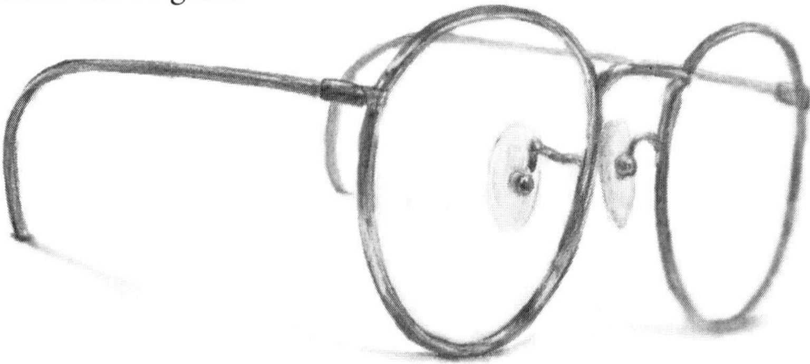

Ocean's Desire

Washing over the stone
raising white frosted hands
up to the sky, to the invisible,
moon — pulling on its senses
in circadian rhythm,
in out, in out,
flinging itself beyond inhibition,
drunk in the power,
the ocean churning below
where I stand, far out of reach,
yet its song draws me
down into the ground,
soaking me into the cliff's
rocky face,
and though I can only
stand and let the water
crash against my sides,
gradually bending my shape
taking the loose sand away
and knowing I cannot embrace
the waves with volcanic
fingers of my own,
I rise against the torrent
welcoming the ocean's
changing power,
calling to the water's
desire to come, to surround,
to be uncontrolled.
I lower my body into
the turquoise tide and declare,
"Drown me down into you!"

Lay Me Down to Sleep

Tonight I lay me
        down to sleep,
praying the Lord
        my soul will keep,

knowing beside
        my soul she'll be,
guiding my steps
        so quietly.

Though she knows
        I don't understand,
even as I sleep
        I feel her hand.

In the night
        she sooths my fear,
holding the light,
        her presence near

and to know
        which road to take
when in the morning
        to her light I wake.

I Know

You don't have to tell me
        you hold me in your heart,
        I can feel it when
        I see you
        looking in my eyes.
You don't have to explain
        that you care.
        I sense it when you
        hold me in your arms
        every time so tight.
You don't have to let me know
        you delight in my spirit,
        I feel it when you
        cup my face
        in your hands.
You don't have to say
        I love you,
I know.

DUELING

Fear,
I challenge you
to a duel.

You walk ten paces
to the left
and I'll walk ten paces
to the right
and whoever manages
to strike out with
their power first

wins.

Alright?

Fear,
where did you go?

AREN'T WE ALL SOULS?

Aren't we all souls?
Subterranean deep,
eternal,
beloved,
dreamed up by God?

Aren't we all precious?
Past the labels, the blades,
beyond the visible,
endlessly creative?

Aren't we all beautiful?
Vibrant colors running,
flaming sunsets
of startling fire,
a vast array of tumbling glory?

We spend so much of ourselves
on hating
yet God does not hate.
God loves every last soul
and aren't we all souls?

Confession

God, I come to you this afternoon
with a confession to make.

I know you love your people,
all people, but I've sat in
many of their cathedrals
and while I am in awe of the
splendor and soaring stone,
I am at the same time saddened
to see so many, now and in times
past, more concerned with
what goes on inside the
walls than without,
more amazed by the architecture
they created
than the God it points to.

I judge them Lord
and I get angry at their
religiosity, their passion
for the rules, how they look,
and if they are doing the "right" thing
completely ignoring the
spirit of the law while your
precious ones who don't fit in
with their idea of "salvation"
assume a warped picture of you
and are turned away.

Give me patience for these
brothers and sisters, Lord,
your reflections, help me see
them with your eyes
and grant me the honor

of battling the lines so I may
know those afraid of you,
helping them in their search
to find unquenchable you,
discovering the connection
you've already forged.

And Lord—
hurry.

Forgiveness in the Daily

Forgiveness is not the road
taken once of an act done
that we need to put away
and get over
but it is *the* road,
the one path to live on
as we inhale into every
moment of every day.
While viewing the crocuses,
a boulder may be
launched onto the trail.
It is our choice whether
to climb over the obstacle
or to keep hitting against
the guilt of ourselves and another
letting it become the new
passion in a poisoned heart.
Yet we kneel down to chip
off stones and aim—
only to perpetuate the pain.
What if instead we continually
washed the grit of a day away,

cleaning our hands
in the waters of imperfection,
knowing we have launched
boulders of our own
and choose instead
to live in the better truth
there are gifts more precious
that we're losing daily,
letting them slip through our fingers
by holding onto an untruth
we have imagined in a false story
while these greater loves,
these gifts God has for us
are trapped underneath
the boulder we refuse to dissolve
because we would rather be right
than forgiven ourselves.
We would rather hold it against
another than admit our own failures.
What do we lose when we don't forgive?
The sight of God.
Covering the divine image in a face
we refuse to see, covering it under
our own self-righteousness,
our own invented anger,
we lose the ability
to see God in ourselves
and in the world around us.
If that is truly so,
why would we *ever*
blindfold our own eyes
and complain of the dark
or keep a rock in our shoe
and try to walk through the pain?
We are so good at creating

our own hells, no one else
needs to do the job for us.
Stand firm in your tenderness.
Don't create a cliff wall
on the road you tread
because you refuse to forgive.
Choose love instead—
    live free.

For a Time

We've made our choices
you and I,
years ago,
we said goodbye
but did not know it
on that day,
some bridges you cross
along the way.
Looking back
at what we've done,
though apart
we both won
a joy, a love,
a time was given,
memories in hand,
life's for living.
I release you now,
all debts are paid,
the time we had
a miracle made.
Perhaps it's a season,
it's not to know,
but I bless you now
as in peace we go.

FINDING CENTER

Sitting in the labyrinth's center
with lights along the trail,
I light a lantern of my own
viewing truth of a larger scale.

Temple of Trees

Entering under your branches
stretching out to greet me
like fingers reaching
out to touch my arms in holy welcome.
You, sacred sentinels,
set apart in timeless ages
standing strong,
my lungs open.
And you — listening to what
my heart cannot bear to speak
as if to assure, "We hear you."
This living cathedral,
towering high overhead
buttressing the wide sky,
wrapping myself around your pillars
held by the rough bark of trees,
the sap of the wood,
drawing me into itself,
soaking into the sinews of my heart,
showing me how to stand
tall and courageous.
I join them there
on the steps of the throne,
shafts of light through open windows,
wisdom of the ages
open to all those who would seek it.
These sacred companions
sharing with me
their divine communion.

Morning Snow

Branches bathed in purity
        reverently resting in awe of your reign.
Below, daffodils bowed in holy white vestments
        before your sacred throne.

Quietly, these gentle blessings fall to the ground—
        living icons walking us into prayer.
You lovingly reveal the world in silent glory
        and my heart kneels down before your grace.

Honoring the Lights

I can lie here all afternoon
watching the sun move through
the shadows of the leaves,
soaking in the brush of the grass,
the berry-rich aroma
cascading into my lungs,
sensing the array of invisible stars
above the azure dome
and holding these
treasured gifts of you
like jewels in my hands
lifting them up to God
here beside me,
honoring these lights that are mine,
glad you've been led along
our trek to teach and share
the Goddess flame within us all
and though I can only glimpse your sun

when the branches wave in the wind,
I still feel its warmth on my skin
nourishing my spirit and laying
its web of rays around my soul.

But if I am unable to raise my head
to rise up and walk out
where I have not yet been,
the light has been for naught.
And if I cannot courageously
hold out my candle
so another may be lit,
I may as well have stayed at home
never to have known the breeze
or the river flowing through my hands.
For a gift must be given,
a treasure must be spent,
and a soul that has first
beheld the blessing
must a blessing be.

MUSES

In solitude
holding your faces
in my gaze,
picturing your smiles
before me—
my fellowship,
my champions,
the unseen craftsman
carving themselves
into this light,
into the words
like inlaid wood
of gems and shells,
red and violet
stained grains together.

Such glory in a face!

And then I understand—
my treasures aren't
the antique desk
or African carved stone
or even the canvases of art
I have created.
But they are you—
resplendent, extraordinary you
in all your celebrations,
your moments of frailty,
your voices of wisdom and grace.
My prize is your presence
even if only in my heart.

But then I feel a hand

laid on my arm,
a gentle touch,
an acknowledgement.
I turn my head
and see a silent
hello in your eyes.

Re-Gifting

Crouching down
underneath

beside another

lifting their load
upon my shoulders
beside their
heavy chests
even if only for
a morning or late evening,

to make lighter
their burden.

I will stand. I will kneel.
I will love
through the strength
in my arms

for I know
what such a gift can mean—

it was first bequeathed to me.

The Deep Knowing

kissing the rose
lips brushing smooth silk petals
of God's breath
showering the deep knowing
with the intoxicating aromas
of worlds beyond
like trying to taste
the snow falling
outstretched tongue
arms caressing out
to wade in the
moonlight pooling
falling on the bed
when his light wakes
me to the brilliance
of the stars
hearing his voice
like the breeze
passing behind
turning my face
to find the whispered voice
calling my name
an invisible hand reaching
up through the water
brushing the hair across
my cheek pulling my
body into the waves
inviting longing dripping
down soaking my soul
raising my chest in a cool
divine
    answering
        breath

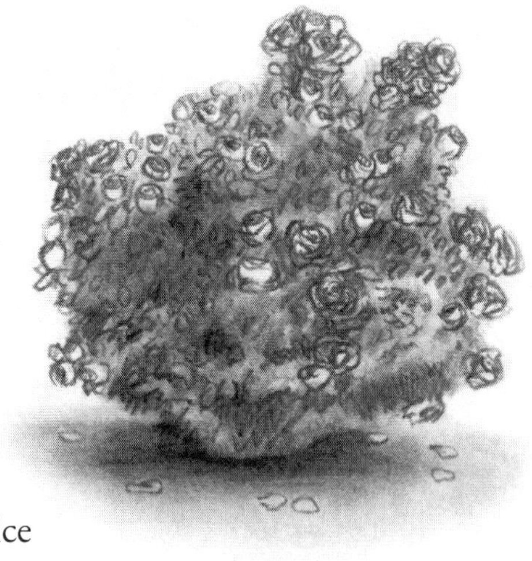

Early Morning Hours

In the early morning hours,
    in the coolness of the air,
before the sun has risen,
        I come to you in prayer.

It's rarely ever easy
    to unfold myself from bed,
but more important than weary sleep
        is to raise my heavy head

to live in first-light moments
    hearing the bird's first call,
listening for you in silence,
        the center of it all.

Oftentimes, I read
    or write with paper and a pen,
or I may curl up in my favorite chair
        to hear what you'll say when

I pour my heart out to you,
    touch your face with outstretched hand,
sharing all the goings on
        cause' you know and understand.

Over time I have discovered,
    this time of you and me,
grounds my spirit in who I am
        helping me to see

the larger picture of this life,
    my soul is wrapped in peace
with a renewed and quiet spirit,
        to the day I am released.

Just One Request

"What do you want?"
    the Lord asked of me.
Pleading, I told him,
    "I want to see
the underneath,
    the sacred to know
between us, around us,
    above and below.
I want within,
    the auras of light,
the colors, the knowledge,
    the grace of your sight."
"Are you prepared
    for what that will cost?
Beyond the boundaries,
    you'll be considered as lost."
"But I will know you
    as you are
this tiny glimpse,
    the universe — a star.
You only matter,
    I am found in your sea.
I'd rather be lost
    than think you far from me."
And so the Lord
    granted my request,
I was given his sight,
    eternal Love expressed.
I could see the unity,
    the bond of creation,
the connection of all,
    divinity in motion.
And sure enough,

lost I am viewed
for thinking, "No boundaries,
the world by God valued."
But I'm not bothered
I walked off the trail,
viewing the world
on a much greater scale.
I can see the fields,
the fences below
and wonder why they exist
for it's the same ground we hoe.
It's the same spirit,
the same One God we love
and yet we pass judgment
putting us above
another who's wrong
so we can be right.
It seems silly to me,
this ruckus, this fight
when there's so little we know
to describe Divine Being,
grasping eternal
infinity reeling.
But I know who has me,
in whose presence I wake
and I know my own self,
knowledge nothing can shake.
Thus people can shout
I'm outside the doors
because I have license from Him
to explore Heaven's floors.
So I speak with God,
I fall to one knee,
"There are wonders around us
for you're all I see."

Above All

Help me make a good choice,
the kind that is best for my soul,
the true person that I am.
Help me make a choice
that will encourage my voice
and nourish my spirit.
Help me make a choice
you would be proud of
because at the end of the day,
yours are the hands I grasp,
yours is the love I yearn for.

Help me know you smile upon
whatever decision I make
and that I can do your work even here,
or wherever I go,
because I am striving to make a difference
telling other people who you really are,
walking with them on their journeys.

But more than any of this,
I want you, just you.
I want to be intimate with you,
to hear you breathing,
feel the warmth of your feet
walking beside my own.
So whatever way I go,
I pray it follows that desire above all,
in all, and through all.
The choice I make is you.

Imago Dei

Our Imago Dei—
the image of God
shining through
and whether we
with the light of God
within us
see ourselves
as a strong, ferocious lion
or a quiet, meek little lamb,
we are mistaken
in our attempts to shine
for God is neither
the lamb nor the lion
but both reside within Her and Him.
The power in our every pore
need not bite
nor should it be hidden away
but be a living, breathing, gentle strength
holding true
to a roaring, passionate love
lifting up a fellow soul.

Empty Hands

Jesus said those who have been
forgiven much, love much.
I say also those who have
lost much, give much.
For it is they who know
the hollow sound of loss,
the ones who remember how
it feels to have empty hands
and they who have realized
empty hands are best.
It is not for them to
keep what they have been given,
but they pass it on,
knowing life can only
be lived when shared,
blessings can only be savored
when others are also wrapped
into the blessing.
Do not hinder them or make
them keep what is held

out in their hands.
It has no value to them,
it holds no sway when others
are in need of what they can give.
Those with empty hands delight
in having something to share.
Then, after your own dark night
when you, too, learn
the value of empty hands,
you will know how to pass these blessings on,
held out in empty hands of your own.

Second Chances

Treading into unknown lands,
trusting for a time outstretched hands
that were once familiar
now a stranger.
Risking all or risking none,
hoping that what once was done
may be brought to come around,
please, I ask you, Lord, surround
this time that's given,
mistakes forgiven.
Please grant us grace
to see your face
hidden behind the hungry hurt,
wash away the held on dirt
from what was said,
an outlook shed.
May we see with eyes anew
the love we continue to share
        in you.

Raising the Sword

Kneeling down before the Lord,
He lays his blade upon my shoulders
in a baptism of voiceless words
under the Heaven's sun.
Calling me to take the place
to which I was born
along with access to the wisdom
to live out such an honor
of wielding the sacred sword
of power and truth,
I lift my hands to accept the gift
as he places the cold metal
into my palms
naming the warrior.

Rising to my feet I stand,
my fingers laid against the blade,
the hilt held firmly in my grip.
Stepping forward,
swinging the blade around
carving a wide arc
into the air,
I raise the tip high to the sky—
Truth to power in synch with my
holy spirit in every stroke
of this embattled wonder.

I know to you it looks like
a pen or a microphone
but to me, to the Lord,
it's the sword of truth
wielded in a prayer.

Brilliant Simplicity

Walking along the cathedral's aisles
soaking in the candles' glow,
the music rising, floating, calling,
the beauty of giving and letting go.

A Voice from the Woods

Out of the dry and quiet wood
comes a voice.
Out of white comes red.
If you stand still and listen,
let your eyes roll over
the arc of wood and stone
out of which is spirit born,
you may hear a voice
calling your name
in the mountains,
along the tree line,
a whisper,
a name you will
never forget.

Spiraling Round

Along life's spiral
coming back around,
a journey begun, out of the old
from the ancient to the new,
reformed, reshaped
from the ashes left behind.
Answers given to the question,
fresh ways open,
weights fallen away
to begin the voyage again.
Gifts let go returned,
an embrace held,
another time to turn the path—
new possibilities arise as we
wind around once more.

The Here and Now

Living in the moment,
cherishing what is before us
while it's here,
rich and creamy—
like peanut butter pie
shared between two,
savored on the tongue
along with the words we share
listened for today
and treasured tomorrow.

All we have is now,
this single moment
and if we, with such limited eyes,
keep looking elsewhere
for what does not exist,
this pie is left uneaten,
the chocolate unenjoyed.

And this friend's company,
the gift God has given today,
will remain a beauty ignored,
a blessing forgotten.

So pull out a chair,
pick up your fork,
and value what you've been
given in the here and now,
not thinking about tomorrow
or yesterday, but present—
living — every last slice of pie,
every delight held, every joy known
until a life is *lived.*

One Hour

One hour to open.
One turn around the face of Mother Time,
to be heard, to enter into the silent sanctuary,
the candles lit in prayer, the dome beckoning
to God above.

One hour for this gift,
these extraordinary moments to sit
in the labyrinth's center
and to raise my hands
in supplication for a minute
of integrity, of the truth
that sets me free.

Just one hour to breathe clean air,
to give voice to what has lain
below the lips of my mouth
like marbles on my tongue,
poured out one after another
as holy water poured out into
the baptismal pool.
I cross myself and fall in head first
knowing the rest will follow
and I am unafraid,
undismayed to feel the water
rush over my head—
finding my courage in feeling my feet
departing the ground.

It's the hour, *the* hour,
and I am open.

Down the Open Road

You are the eternal rock
to which I hold, the solid
foundation on which I stand.
Though life swirls about me
in turbulence and uncertain feeling,
you are here, present, constant,
walking beside me with an open ear
and wise words of counsel and power.
May I continue turning to you,
knowing from you comes my strength,
that no matter what happens
or what new twists this road may take,
you will always show me how
to take the next steps,
run when needed,
and that I can turn to you always,
my heart staid in your presence
as we go down the open road.

Walking with the Mystics

Walking among you,
unseen companions,
our spirits mingling together
as I join your choir
singing in harmony,
taking strength from your voices,
your presence nearby
like being wrapped in the warmth
of a friend at rest beside me.
The intimacy of hearts united
speaking to my soul,
reminding my body that though
your words first birthed in ages past,
still you're here, teaching, guiding,
letting me know I do not
walk this way alone.
But you who know
those indescribable
moments with Christ,
those wonders, that view
of all-consuming love,
I know you welcome me into your arms,
taking me into your eternal company
and creating a place for my soul.

Massaging Hands

Every soul is a piece of the other—
skin touching skin,
cells coming to know the hands
caressing their smooth frame,
learning to trust
one to another,
yea, even love,
to mingle with
another life force,
acknowledging one's part of another
that no man is indeed an island
but part of one breath
and that when those hands
are laid one on another,
they are laid on the heart.

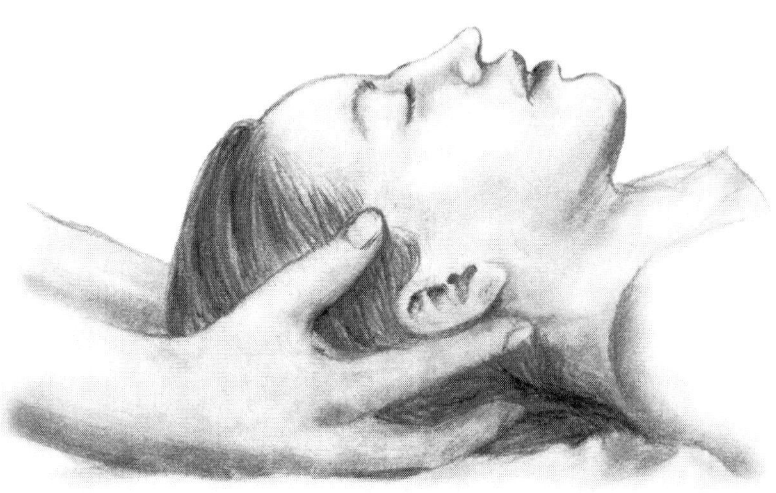

When the Moon is High

When the moon is high
I step into the boat floating
upon the sleeper's sea
and sail into the dusk of night
with a prayerful hope you
will meet me among
the lapping waves
glistening starlight upon
the mystic waters.
This melodious darkness
where you meet the soul
in truth more real than
the dust under the sun,
more perceptible than
the road I trod when I wake,
this is the song my heart sings,
the call of every desire that is you.
So every time I lay my head,
I hold the cherished wish
you will open my eyes
as I close them.
That you will take my outstretched
hand in a place I can see not,
speak to me words clear in the deep
so I can truly see,
to sense you when the morning comes.

Web of Light

I see the shadow on your face,
the darkness weighing in your eyes.
The look lays itself down in my heart
for my soul recognizes where it has been,
recognizes the sensation of standing
on the edge of a chasm, black and deep,
the abyss yawning open before your feet.
You take a step back yet are pulled forward
dropping to your knees in pain.
How much can you lose
before you lose yourself?
How much can be taken before
there's nothing left to take?
The look is startling
for I see where I have walked
and I can see where you are.
Once wondering why people
let me walk that road alone,
falling down the sides of loss,
why they ostensibly abandoned me to the deep.
But now I know only we can drink our own cup
and only we can eat the bitter bread set before us.
We cannot fully know another's distress,
to fully understand how another tastes life,

but we can walk beside them in it,
we can help support them on the way.
And now I see how people were there,
silently looking into the dark shadow
with me and bringing light
and I realize they did not abandon me
but were there alongside me
just as we now stand there with you.
Though we cannot take the grief away,
though we must let the storm howl,
the rain fall, and the wind lash,
we will not let it drown you.
God will not let it drown you.
The water may cover your head,
the waves may toss you,
but we will hold a thread of light,
a divine string threading through the darkness
for you to hold onto throughout the night.
As long as this affliction is yours to bear,
we will walk the journey with you.
We will help you find your balance once again
and remind you of the great strength within.
You see, we are a web of light,
an interconnected body where when one falls,
the rest help them up, again and again.
It moves around the circle and as each person
takes their journey, we walk with them
and the dark and the web of light
transforms us all, from glory to glory,
from me to you to others who hold the strings,
who offer support and
receive support in their turn.
And that great strength within,
the one we call God,
She who has woven us all into this web together,
She will support us, me, you, every one of us,
through this web of light eternally
threaded through Her hands.

Voice of My Soul

I have lived as a mute
though can now at last
speak forth all the openings
cascading inside me,
all the water held up
behind the rock wall
covered in moss,
now free to pour
down the mountain,
carving up a path of its own.
I am free to jump and sing!
To cry those tears
through pencil lead,
to wipe my face in
those dirty pink eraser bits
and when at last I'm
exhausted once again,
when I've finished
pouring out this cavern
of heart holdings,
I can flood the valley
watching the waves
cleanse the land anew.

These Heroes...

...whose battles are their own—
by their choices or another's,
the tumbler of amber beer,
burning cigarettes, white powder,
standing beside graves of grief
far too young to pay the bill.

Gazing into the eyes of
those whose sorrow has
carved into their lives
the wisdom of open grace,
open arms, the strength
of marble, soft lines
upholding a brilliant form.

They are the pursuers,
the givers, the lovers,
enfolding seeds into
soils of verdant earth,
honoring the desire to grow,
to run, to flow free.

They are the dreamers,
exploring the edge of what is.
They are the laughers, the demented,
treading glibly through the profane,
tossing the sacred, crossing the lines,
showing themselves in neon colors,
boldly unique, courageously *them*.

I gaze upon these figures standing
proudly, emanating light.
And this regard I hold,

the deep respect, the love
for these heroes,
these teachers, beloved friends,
the women with whom I walk
and ride the waves,

I think on you—
    and shine.

Sacred Space

To give the quiet gift
    is rarely very loud,
a silent, sometimes sacred thing
    rarely picked out from the crowd.

But held in open hands
    that are steady, sure, and true,
this quiet gift is given
    when I am near to you.

And it truly doesn't matter
    if you realize it or know
the change in space around you,
    how the peaceful seems to grow.

The gift will still be given,
    the effect is yet the same,
a sanctuary of quiet love
    in spirit if not in name.

GIFTING YOU

Perceiving the Divine in others,
God's eyes looking out from their faces,
receiving the individual's weaknesses,
not holding them in focus
but keeping sharp the gift,
the gradual unwrapping over time
of unveiling the joy of the words,
the beauty of a smile beloved
and though these moments are
cherished, held most dear
with open, grateful hands,
they do not diminish
the strength in my own step,
the power in my own voice
or the steel rod of
confidence in my back.

Nay, they add to the treasure!
Rubies upon pearls,
the gift multiplies
as we refine one another,
carving impressions of ourselves
into the hearts of our companions,
the figure of a Lord most adored
taken seed in new soil.

And if I rejoice at the sight of your hands
it is because my own hands
recognize the spirit that directs them,
the same spirit moving me,
gifting you.

Hello and Goodbye

Taking grief as our walking companion,
we search for a road of clarity,
somewhere to grasp the loss
as we want something
that will last forever
because nothing stays
in our tightly gripped hands
but everything that makes us
is lost, everything that shapes us
was never meant to stay.

The hand may carve the sculpture
but moves on to other forms
as the river digs into its banks
but goes on to join the sea.

It is not for us to keep the gift
but to join the flow,
from one person to another,
taking the water, passing the cup,
knowing the goodbye will come
while cherishing the touch of the hands today.
We are nourished by the light
then the night soaks in around us,
a night of loving and letting go
before a new light is birthed tomorrow.

For All the World

Stepping in the forest's sun,
God beside, around, above,
speaking to the world he made
of her fierce, unconditional love.

Deeper Peace

Once again with weary head,
I lay my face upon your knee.
Once again with tender hand,
you caress the soul of me.

I feel your gentle finger
trace the lines upon my cheek,
then I look into your eyes
and wait for you to speak.

But the words I expect for you to say
never reach my ear.
Instead you hum a melody,
softly, loving, clear.

You give the gift of presence
and the deepest peace of you
while you sit with me in the midst of love,
letting your light shine through.

Five Minutes

Spending five minutes
to start the day,
time with God
before finding my own way.

But God does not want
my little bit of time,
a wisp of a moment,
a tug on the line.

He doesn't want me
to stop and say,
"Oh, now my five
minutes are up today!"

"I'll talk to you later God,
tomorrow I'll return.
We'll sit down together
and I'll listen and learn."

God wants our lives,
all the moments of the day,
sharing our time together
hearing what the other would say.

He's with us as we breathe,
He holds us as we sleep,
communing with his spirit,
we know his presence deep.

In the Roots

Rolling onto my
back in the grass
feeling the earth
curve up in my spine
spread eagle upon
the sloping bank,
the balmy breeze
waves warm greetings
to a contented face
raising eyes to
gaze at the leaves,
lemon green,
a thousand ears
taking in the sweet
sound of stillness
as the sun filters
through to lay upon
my body at rest
soaking in the roots
of the trees,
cradled in the heady
aroma of rich loam
and the rocking
of the soil breathing
in the swinging rhythm
of the inborn memory
from which my body comes
and returns for
wordless connection
and a peace
unique
and whole.

It Matters

In the space between words,
you act like every moment
matters because it does
and I love you for it.
You willingly enter into a
world of wonder, welcoming
the joys and angst lying
before you, taking them into
yourself, holding them for
others, like a sentinel, silently
standing beside the way.
And though this world is stilled,
though at its core I hardly
hear the breath of the wind,
I sink into silence and know
the absence of words—
speaking forth far more,
holding greater power
than all the trees standing tall
in the pulsating wind,
changing the clouds,
like the lives transformed
in every moment
because it matters.

The Anchor Always Holds

Out on the troubled waters,
in the darkness of the night,
there was a ship out tossing
guided by the light.

Though the waves were high
and towered overhead,
the rain lashed down in torrents
as death before her spread.

The sails were torn and tattered,
the mast was cut in two,
sailors lost their courage
as hope from them withdrew.

The seamen raised their frightened cries,
they cried their pain-filled tears,
they screamed and shouted to the wind
but it only intensified their fears.

Thunder made her mighty roar
and lightening struck the bow.
Just as it seemed that all was lost,
heavy fog overtook the prow.

Soon the ship was cast in shadows,
the boat could not be seen,
the sailors were no longer heard
above the frothy green.

A veil had been drawn around them
through the thickening haze.
Though the storm blew on,
no message could be raised.

Then as the dawn of morning
broke out across the sea,
out came a ship of splendor,
shining for all to see.

The sails were white and flying,
the paint was clean and bright,
majestic stood the Captain
who had seen them through the night.

The sailors were out dancing
out on the deck with glee,
though now they understood
what it was like upon the sea.

They sang a song of wisdom
with insight from above,
guided by the stars overhead
and an anchor cast in love.

Their faces were filled with light
and the roar was now their song.
It was the one the captain taught them
to guide their spirits strong.

"He knows the way through the cleansing storm
and what blessings it can bring.
He will pull the oars beside you
and encouragement He will sing."

"His hand is held out to you,
untold grace He will unfold,
and when you can hear nothing else,
He shouts, 'The anchor always holds!'"

Dust Baths

Ducking her beak into the dirt
throwing sod onto the feathers
covering her back,
stretching wings, golden brown,
clucking the soil,
her own plump body
washing the earth.

Beside her in the mud,
digging your fingers
and planting your flowers,
turning the dark clods,
breaking them up,
the evidence under your nails
streaked on your face
as you're pulling up roots
and putting down your own.

Then at last I understand—
you who sit beside
this bird of the earth,
who sinks into the ground
planting yourself thus,
whose feet are bare,
naked and brown,
caked with the dust
under your heels,
you too, come to the soil
taking a bath in the dirt
to wash your soul anew.

Smell of the Roses

There are roses by my walk
that you will never see.
There are things I'll never tell you
for you are far from me.
The life you once invested in
has now come into bloom,
the path I've taken since we left
is filled with dancing room.
So when I smell the roses,
my thoughts often turn toward you,
wondering if you'll even see
the change you never knew.
But I suppose it doesn't matter,
there are greater goals above,
it's the life I share with God, I know,
His direction, peace, and love.

Sneaky Fingers

I am looking for that last ingredient,
the last bit to be dropped into the bowl.
The dough is goopy, where is the flour?
The dough is dry, where is the water?
Baking soda, nope — already in.
Vanilla? Sweet enough.
Cinnamon, pushed aside.
Nutmeg is quickly passed by.
Maybe in the back of the cupboard,
forgotten in a corner
waiting to be used.
Perhaps I already put it in
or God dropped the portion
in behind my back. (?)
She, smiling, dressed in a
green African wax print apron,
sneaky fingers with red nail polish
grabbing a jar when
I wasn't looking, giving it
a sift or two—
her black face grinning,
white teeth like an oven
light giving radiance
to what is soon to be baked within
where it might not be hidden
but seen, admired.
Maybe she, with stretched
earlobes dangling silver rings,
while I poured the white-churning milk,
a half-cup, it must be just right (!),
threw in a dash of chocolate powder,
a couple of raisins (who's counting?)
and a handful of butterscotch chips.

Swaying her wide hips,
giving the salt a shake
to the rhythm of a hard rock tune,
(is God allowed to do that?)
I rummage through the measuring cups
for that one-eighth teaspoon,
but she gives the batter a stir,
a bit of this, a dollop of that,
a final swirl of caramel,
pouring the contents into the pan,
licking the spoon with a relish
rivaling that of a fine French wine.
She slides the confection onto the rack,
waiting in the heat, I'm impatient
until the top is a beautiful golden brown.
Reaching down, I lift my fork—
Mmm…
See? Just right.

Reaching Back

Reaching back, your small
hands find their way into mine
as we bound along this wooded trail.
Pointing out the rounded mushrooms
or how to take five deep breaths,
moments I would have otherwise missed
if not for your wonder-filled smile.
While dabbling in the stream,
catching the drips of a waterfall
or taking a dive into the lake,
you open up worlds in my eyes
where anything can and *does* happen.
Where it's okay to get married
to a stuffed dog — three times—
and plastic food tastes best
in quilted bear caves
as we chase the leaves
and make angels in the snow.

And I can't help but think
though I am the one with greater age,
the one who has tried to teach you
about the love of God and good character,
it is I who have learned,
I'm the one who's changed,
the one who can't help but see
the joy of the Lord
in your hello-grin calling my name.
Beautiful, beautiful you—
my prayer warrior, my friend,
reaching back to me,
taking *my* hands,
as we bound along this wooded trail.

Leadership

Words echoing, "You are a leader,"
still reverberate around inside
like water rushing around a stream
nourishing every seed, every blade of grass,
long after you first spoke them.

And though the honor of leading,
of serving, has carved out
new layers of light
in who God equipped me to be,
you named something in that moment,
recognized a skill already lived out:
the influence on those around me,
opening the way for me
to see it in myself.

And now, feeling this mantle
of headship settled around my neck,
from God's hands through yours,
fully claimed as my own,
owning the responsibility,
I stand tall in the courage to wear it,
to walk with strength under
the yoke held in tandem with Christ.

Kneeling under the gift of stepping forth,
I hold to the integrity of character,
the willingness to speak when others are silent,
the intrinsic knowledge we all hold equal value
even as I make needed decisions affecting many.
With grace I wield this power as you once taught,
this task for which I was chosen—
        being a leader: compassionate, strong and true.

Tramp for the Lord

In honor of Corrie Ten Boom

Walking the lands of this world,
a bag slung over my back,
my feet itching for adventure—
new places — voicing new words,
who knows where I might next go?

The savannahs of Africa,
or the streets of a Belgium city.
Perhaps a port where slaves
were once sold to speak on the taking
of a freedom too vast to understand
on a simple piece of paper.
I might call out in the markets of India
or sit at table with friends in Moscow.
It could be I'll sail the ocean
to learn Spanish in La Paz
towered over by the Chilean mountains.
Who knows from where
the invitation might next come?

But my bag is packed,
my voice is ready,
my feet eager to set off down the road,
down that unknown way—
sliding down mountains
or running along canals
to catch the next train.

I'm willing to find my way
through the continents,
backpack at the ready heading off to...
Well, who knows?
I'm a tramp.
For the Lord.

Love Can Never Die

A mother holds her little child
gently in her arms,
pain fills her eyes,
the baby cries
as she softly sings this song:
"Take care my love,
I cannot stay,
I have to say goodbye."
She leaves the newborn baby
in the arms of God,
hoping that he'll guide her
in the life she now walks toward.

Now the baby is a girl,
strong in love and living,
though deep inside
there's still a hole where
her mother's voice is singing:
"Take care my love,
I cannot stay,
I have to say goodbye."

Mother, daughter reunite,
a rebellious teen in hand.
Pain and joy stroll together
as they travel distant lands.
This young woman decides to go,
seeking her path out in the world,
finding strength in the song she's heard,
sung so long ago.
"Take care my love,
I cannot stay,
I have to say goodbye."

Now a mother with
young women of her own,
she travels with her siblings,
joy found now fully known.
Yet still the tears
fall from her face,
she is back where she began,
seeing her mother leave again
as she holds her dying hands.
She thinks of all
the time they lost,
and the time they
have been given,
the gift they found
in one another,
and the lessons they
learned in living.
Then as she bows her head to hear
her mother's whispered words,
for one last time the mother sings
the ending she's never heard.
"Take care my love,
I cannot stay,
I have to say goodbye.
But I will always
be with you
for love can never die."

The Unanswered Question

God, what do you sound like?
Every time I think I know
you run off laughing
and I never hear you the same.
It must be a singular sound
like the wind whistling,
singing through trees to wide open sky
or a deer's bounding leap
taking away my ability to say
you remind me of the babbling brook—
always changing in my ears
but made of the same rich earth,
the same nourishing flow of life
as you have always been.

I must tell you it's disconcerting
for I'm trying to figure you out
and then another endless
network of trails opens before me
to explore with courageous curiosity.
You never end.

But if I could hear you,
would I stop searching?
If I knew your one voice,
would I recognize it anywhere else?
And so I'm climbing over the logs and wading in streams
in search of this unanswered question
knowing you are best heard in the unpredictable
where hope scales the mountains
and love runs wild.

I hear you.

About the Author

Sarah Katreen Hoggatt has been writing for over twenty years and is the author of several books and numerous articles. She is a freelance writer, international speaker, editor, and spiritual director with a passion for ministering to fellow souls. She holds a Master of Arts degree in Christian Ministry and a Certificate of Spiritual Formation and Discipleship from George Fox Evangelical Seminary in addition to her Bachelor of Science degree from Oregon State University. Sarah currently makes her home in Salem, Oregon where she revels in hiking, dragon boating, acting in theatre, and photography. She is passionate about living her life as a gift.

For more information, see her blog:
WalkingTheSea.blogspot.com.

About the Illustrator

Erin Kays has been drawing most of her life. She is a third year undergraduate student at George Fox University, double majoring in Graphic Design and Studio Arts. Erin enjoys exploring charcoal, water color painting, and pencil work in the traditional arts. In the digital field she loves applying traditional techniques to create art in Adobe Photoshop. She sings and plays piano, guitar, violin, bass guitar, and recently has picked up the ocarina. When she is not living at the University, she lives in West Linn, Oregon. In the next couple of years she wants to write and illustrate a children's book.

Erin thanks her parents, sister, and brother for their support and encouragement throughout this process. To her friends she says, "You have been amazing and I thank you for your inspiration!"

Other Books by Sarah Katreen Hoggatt

Learning to Fly $12.95

Have you ever felt the longing inside your heart to explore new heights of sky, to rise on lifted wings? Have you ever longed for more than what you know? In her first book of poetry, Sarah shares her gift as a writer by revealing a journey of learning to fly in a world full of challenges and immeasurable joy. Her honest and candid spirit gives the reader a sense of deeper vision and intimacy with God compelling you to discover flying lessons within yourself.

In His Eyes $12.95

Held within the pages of *In His Eyes*, the continued story of *Learning to Fly*, is an exploration of the miraculous, ever-growing relationship the soul shares with God. Through her experience of learning how God is passionately beside us in every moment of our lives, in all the joys and difficulties we discover, Sarah compels the reader to lift up their face, soak in the sight of the stars, and to see God's eyes returning their gaze.

Encountering the Holy $6.00

Christmas time is so busy that spending time reflecting upon the miracle of Jesus is often pushed down to the bottom of our lists. *Encountering the Holy* creates needed holy space by reflecting on special moments and things to ponder every day of the Advent season. Through a variety of topics, Sarah Katreen Hoggatt brings forth a fresh look at the season and through personal stories of her own, brings new light to becoming more aware of the Holy One of Israel.

Order at SpiritWaterPublications.com